Romar Press

Stephenville, Texas

2018

ISBN-13: 978-0692136836 (Romar Press)

ISBN-10: 0692136835

First edition

Copyright © 2018 Marilyn Robitaille

Cover art and design © 2018 Marilyn Robitaille

All rights reserved. This book and its contents may not be used or reproduced in any form without the author's prior written consent except for fair use in reviews and/or scholarly considerations.

With special acknowledgments:

"Moonlight and a Movie" and "The Expatriates" first appeared in *Langdon Review of the Arts in Texas, Volume 3,* (2006-2007);

"A Million Miracles" (as "Promises"); "We Two, Us" (as "Connected") first appeared in *Langdon Review of the Arts in Texas, Volume 9,* (2012-2013);

"Sicily, Sicily, Sicily," "Let's Suppose You Know," and "Of a Moment Wild" first appeared in *Writing Texas, Vol. 1* (Lamar University Press, 2013-2014);

"A Fine Blue Stone," "For My Aunt Flossie," and "A Frank Sinatra Sighting in New York City" first appeared in *Her Texas: Story, Image, Poem & Song* (Wings Press, 2015);

"Monrose in August" first appeared in *Texas Weather: An Anthology of Poetry, Short Fiction, and Nonfiction* (Lamar University Press, 2016);

"45th Anniversary" first appeared in *Langdon Review of the Arts in Texas, Volume 14,* (2017-2018).

Picasso quotation attributed by Tate Modern in exhibit and brochure of *Picasso 1932 – Love, Fame, Tragedy* to a conversation with Daniel Kahnweiler in *'Entretiens avec Picasso au sujet des Femmes d'Alger,' Aujourd'*hui, September 1955. Cited in M.L. Bernadac and A. Michael (eds.), *Picasso propos sur l'art*, Paris, 1998. p. 72.

All for Charlie

Not by Design

Fifty Poems and Images

by

Marilyn Robitaille

Prefatory Remarks

The editorial I wrote in *Langdon Review of the Arts in Texas*, Volume 8 (2011-2012) attempts to explain the mystical, mysterious artistic process with its transcendent, at times almost accidental, elements. Given the manner in which *Not by Design: Fifty Poems and Images* came into existence, what I said then certainly applies:

> Everything's a nothing, then a misty glimmer, then a moment drawn from memory or some space beyond. A chance encounter sparks a thought and suddenly a poem takes flight. A dream occurs, giving rise to a surprise melody. Scraps of wood conform in arcs and wings, configuring into geometric loveliness. A space of white draws in color to capture some secret essence. One camera click distills time, rendering the scene permanent and forever. A story long buried, its roots twisted deep, emerges, spiraling to the surface like those time-lapse pictures of a flower in bloom. Magic, all of it, and it is here in tangible form now, ink on paper, a thing to be reckoned with. Read. Absorbed.

And let's not forget Picasso's statement, the very one accentuated by the Tate Modern in the recent Picasso exhibit. The curators placed it so starkly on the wall, I had to pause and take a picture of it:

> 'You start a painting and it becomes something altogether different. It's strange how little the artist's will matters.'
> Pablo Picasso

All of this to explain that this book bears very little resemblance to what I first imagined it would be. It began as an anniversary chapbook to celebrate forty-five years of marriage to Charlie Robitaille. He knew I had a filing system that defied all logic, and if I died before I printed everything and gave him a hard copy, all would be lost. So I set out for this to be a poetic homage to marriage. For lack of a better title, I started referring to it as *Blissful*. Charlie never really took to that title. I don't know what inspired me to embark on the art, but once I decided to illustrate the poems, I was a woman obsessed. I wanted to capture an idea, a circumstance, an essence, or at times a literal component of the poem – often something in that twilight between dreamscape and reality. Being a word person, I agonized over the organization. Occasion poems go together; the ones with an overwhelming sense of place can hang in one section; people poems created a weird community; then those narratives sort of felt unhinged; and what about the ones that didn't fit any of my pigeon holes. I made the effort, and then laid out the canvas counterparts in order, five across, ten down to make a giant collage. All was not well, but I soldiered on.

Then a miracle occurred. My dearest friend happens to be my sister-in-law Catherine Seabring. She has an artistic flair like non-other, works miracles with interior design, and makes her living as a professional organizer. When she saw the giant conglomeration of canvases on my floor, she went a little apoplectic. "Why do you have these in this order?" were the first words out of her mouth.

"They're in the order of the poems," I explained, "But something's not working. What order should they be in?"

"Why are the poems determining the order of the art? Let the art determine the order of the poems," she said.

"Have at it!" I told her with an edge of excitement I was trying to stifle. Could it be that simple? In less than ten minutes, she had divided the canvases into two manageable groupings five by five each. You'll see those at the beginnings of the two sections. In a flurry brought on by the artist's eye, she rearranged the art. Suddenly, I saw things I didn't see before. Bold and bright didn't distract from more somber images. The groupings maximized colors, textures, and contrasts. She was brilliant. Magic happened right before my eyes.

As I grabbed my manuscript and started reorganizing the poems, I proclaimed, "Well, this is not by design." And the title came marching in. So there you have it: a poem about a funeral comes up next to one about a birth. Happy poems give way to sad or angry ones. A mood poem about Sicily lives next to a high school memory poem. This has been a journey to celebrate the years with the man I love. I'm glad his sister stepped in with her brand of magic.

June 28, 2018

TABLE OF CONTENTS

Part I

Mustang in the Park 1970 3
First Christmas 5
A September Birthday Wish For you . 7
A Fine Blue Stone 9
Baby Lovely 11
She Waits 13
Montrose in August 15
A Frank Sinatra Sighting in New
    York City 17
In Grace and Love 21
A Little Crazy 25
Medical Destiny 27
Damn the Norwegians 29
Gaze from the Back Forty 31
To the Fullest 33
We Two, Us 35
A Couple Observed in Winter 37
Of an Island Sicily 41
That Other Name 45
Your poem 49
Advice at Twenty-five 51
Lyrical Hope 55
Let's suppose you know 57
Tupelo, Oh Tupelo 59
A Million Miracles 63
Winning Ticket 65

Part II

For Dylan: On the Demise of a Very
    Good Cat 69
Oasis Love 73
Just There 77
Father-Daughter 79
Starlight in Guadalajara 83
Obscure Blessings 85
The Wise Woman of the Rock 89
The Expatriates 93
Tribal Love 95
Birth 99
Fair Fever 101
Real Action 103
Sunlit On the Beach at St. Tropez .. 107
One 111
Spaces in a Connecticut Road 113
Of a Moment Wild on Port Aransas
    Beach 115
Ethiopian Friend 119
Virgin 121
Prunes 123
45th Anniversary 127
Epithalamium 131
Strawberries and Smooth Jazz 135
For My Aunt Flossie 139
Betrayal 143
Moonlight and a Movie 145

Part I

Mustang in the Park 1970

We are contortionists

My leg over your thigh over your arm

Your arm over my neck under my chin

Rising heights the moment full

Windows fog, we don't care

We are parkers in the night

In the city park of Stephenville

We play a different kind of baseball

You are my fly ball. I am your home base.

We are wicked. Kissing. Steaming windows

My skin smooth against the black backseat

Your breath warm and oozing wonderful

Breathe in. Breathe out. Breathe in.

This is youth defined

But we don't know it

First Christmas

Away in a manger another baby
Long time ago, magic in the sky
Now you're here, all beaming, ours
You must have met that other child
In brilliant light and mystery
You tell me in your glisting eyes
Toothless laugh and in a million moments
When I am still and listening
Not often, not often to sit and rock
And watch the sky and note the blue
The clouds, the banks of angels, songs
You hear as steady as your heart beat
We mark this day with special time
Gifts and cheer, hugs all around
You take it in on gossamer so slight
We won't know the rhyme or reason
Your moment yours across the moon
Above the clouds into the essence of it all
To know the innocence, the beauty
Remind me to make the journey last
To make it round the seasons on the wind
Remembering, remembering the reason
For it all and note the day the babe was
Born in innocence, your co-conspirator
And in health and healing, beauty and in love.
Christmas, Christ and Christmas Christ
And the babe, on this day a child was born
And you are one with love and ours

A September Birthday Wish for You

I hope you howl at tonight's full moon

Take liberties with wine, women, and song

Even if you're out of order or off key

Scratch where it itches

Don't wear a neck tie or pressed pants

Behold the glory of your gray hair

Bask in the full bright light of good company

Bow to the gods and be grateful

Remember your day with wild pleasure

Shun work and escape all drudgery

Seek forgiveness even if you don't deserve it

Dance to wild abandon with two left feet

Hear music in the sky and stars

Turn up the volume all the way

Take joy in being unruly and ungoverned

Make memories for the next fifty birthdays

Leave no stone unturned or, if it suits, stay stoned

Be reckless, but don't be a wreck

Go with the flow, saying ommm

Zen to you in all things big and small

On this the day of your birth so long, long ago

Love your tribe and know that you are loved

A Fine Blue Stone

Not by design, but quite by accident, I am here

Little more than a stone's throw

From Hòa Lò Prison, Hanoi Hilton

Time heaped upon time for suffering

More than brick and mortar all entombed

The whispers in all languages of the men

Whose wings were clipped, whose souls sucked dry

Pleas to heaven and the sun, evermore a memory

In this dark, demon-place time turns in upon itself

With cold walls and shadows smelling of the grave

I withstand the moment with the of touch of stone

A smooth, blue rock made perfect by a hand

Who knows so well the moments of this country

The smell of fear, gun-metal green, break of day

Across the fields whose smoke-filled haze

Ignites the glow and brings it all together

All that he is beyond this place, he fashions out a perfect jewel

I wear it as a talisman to keep me safe, a token peace

Around my neck, one perfect, blissful blue stone

All that it means so clear now that the burn has cleared

In reverence to the ghosts, a fine blue stone

Beauty defined and defended

In Hanoi

Baby Lovely

You are our blessed event
Our baby lovely in splendor shining
Beyond the earthly limits
Come breezing down to earth
In golden goodness innocent
Here in life's muddy stuff
That we have come to know
We being here a long, long time
Planet earth with all its trials and
Heartaches. It's what we know, know best
Beyond our problems, we see the hope
We go to work and say our prayers
Always busy with unimportant things
So vague and blurry we can't remember
Yesterday. You're not so jaded in your
Essence, you are new and fresh
Alive in radiance, but wise beyond this day
You take it in as if you know a secret
Smile, laugh out loud, raise those eyebrows
You captured us in minutes and we are
Slaves to your loveliness. All of it a mystery
That we won't take for granted.
And if we do, let this poem remind us
Of your magic, of your love so absolute.
In its perfection, its infinity complete.

She Waits

She waits in the dark
In the cold night air
It cuts like a knife
Blows leaves at her feet
Chills to the bone
He promises to arrive at the gate
        in seventeen minutes
Precision like a surgeon's scalpel

She wills him to be on time
Then
Lights of a car rainbowing
        across the street
She cannot know for sure
Feeling his stony hardships
Knowing his needful pain
Immersed, she is there for him
Standing alone, here now
Waiting in the cold night air
This moment
Slicing life in increments

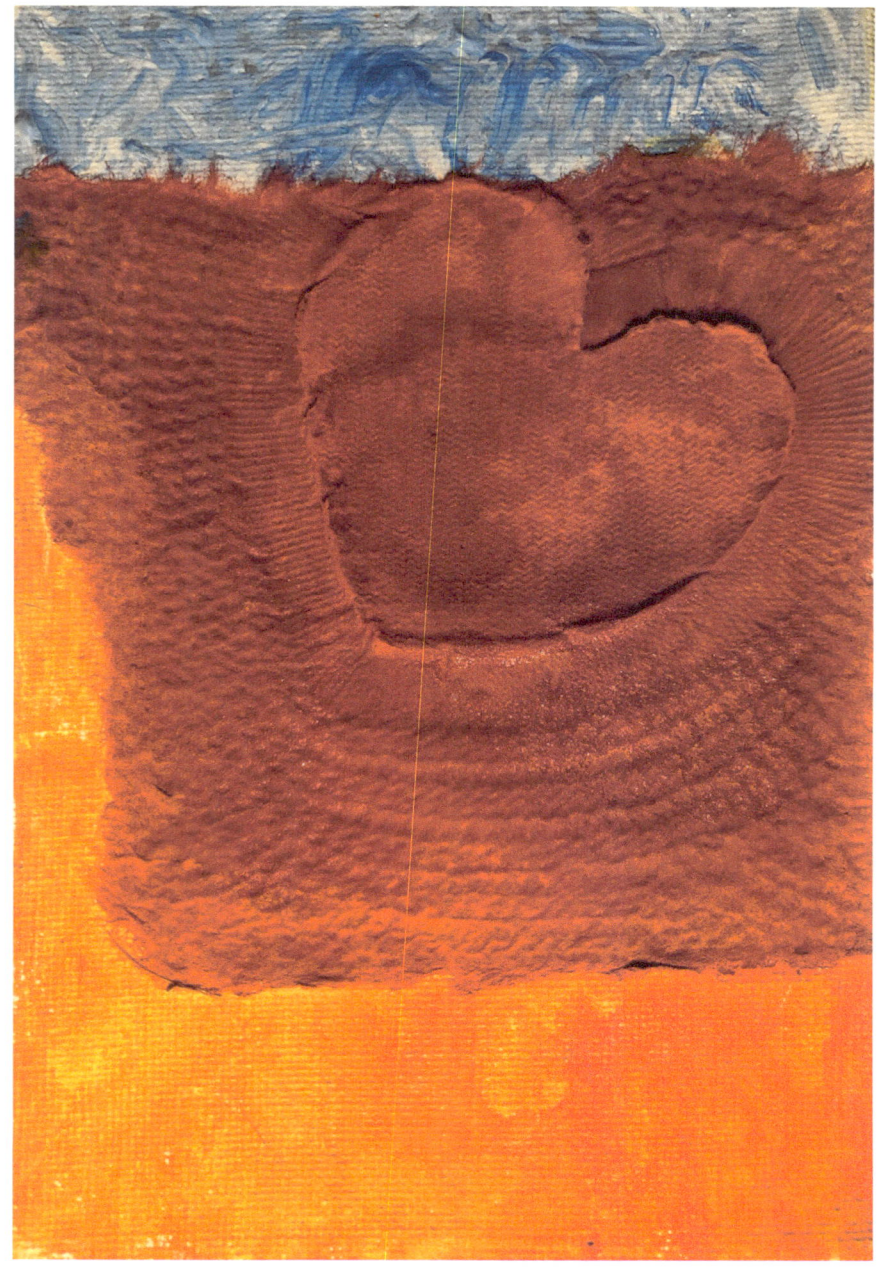

Montrose in August

She is white hot

Naked, alone

Skin against the sheets

Sweat pooling

Midnight in August

One single window

Open to the city

Montrose in Houston

    her territory

No air, only notes of jazz

Gathering like a storm

To soothe her

She dreams of slow rain

Then realizes her mistake

Texas summer is a demon

Dancing on her grave, laughing

She gathers herself

Sits on the side of her bed

   to think, head in hands

She is in hell, fires burning

Wishing for home, for Montana mountains

Wishing for cobalt blue and breezes

Wishing for a liquid lover to cool her down

He will not come

This is August in Montrose

Heat

A Frank Sinatra Sighting in New York City

It rained that cold afternoon in New York City
Gun gray skies met gloomy sidewalks
Landscapes washed away the city's color.
In a blur of steel leaves, damp and dripping
We walked through Central Park

Bundled you in your black coat, me cocooned in white
We looked like companion penguins
Wobbling down the street against the wind
It's a damp cold, you'd said, and I agreed.
We need a strong drink — Irish whiskey, you'd said
      And I agreed again.

Rosie O'Grady's bar the sign alleged, so
      We went in, shelter against the cold
Both inside and out.
We started toward a table, then gave pause
The bar looked more New York
Polished gravity against the years where all
Those Irish whiskeys turned saints into sinners
      Or maybe, sometimes, the other way around.

We settled in, hoping to hide our tourist otherness
      meaning business, ordering two shots
Downing them like they were our last
Because maybe they were we thought

        gasping against the burn
Precisely then, just then the door opened wide
And we saw him standing there, Old blue eyes
Mr. Frank Sinatra and his entourage
Advancing in tuxedo regiment to Rosie's back room.
He smiled and waved like the Queen of England
As they marshaled through the bar

You stood up, smiled, said hi, Frank like old friends.
I seized pen, then napkin for an autograph
Thrusting them with my best Texas smile
and he looked at us
        Bluely
Then he was gone, all gone and the back door closed.

He might as well have been
        A stranger in the night for all its worth.
The door to Rat Pack heaven closed to us
Since we weren't canonized.
Frankly speaking, I hollered out, thanks for nothin', Frank.
Then we rallied up our strength to meet
New York City's damp, gray cold now
To the depths of our good Irish whiskey

In Grace and Love

We measure out a life in goodness tempered
Beyond what most imagine to be possible
One man who always had a smile and understood
The light fantastic, who knew the best in all of us
Who never had a word unkind and never fostered one
A man who worried with the fates that he stay in God's favor
When doctrines of his church and faith might ask
Great things of him to discern the truth and know it.

His stories melted over us until we felt the flow:
His rag doll lost meant hope in new spring
A watermelon thief rejoiced knowing summer sweetness
A Navy boy met with war time challenges and
Heard the toll of Big Ben booming out the time
Look for my footprints, he said, when you hear the chime
And we did, posing for the photographs and wondering
At all those London ghosts he shared with us:
A child in red patent shoes, a gallon drum of marmalade,
A ship of metal gray, and his dress whites.
Anchors away awhile.

What we know of your life we've come to celebrate
And think about the legacy you've left
To see the world all better than it is, but what it might be.
Your light left brighter to burn through us because
We loved you and the promise you inspired.
I can't sum up the riches of it all or find a way to say it

The years you sang the gospels loud and clear
The days you sold the cars and won awards
Made vitamins and sold the calves and did the deals
Your Lions Club dedications and the speeches
You are all of it and bigger in your love
We know your light and thank you for it
You brought us to the fountain's source
Inspiration's muse summoned by your blessing
A life well lived in grace and love
And that's the best of it

A Little Crazy

You are two
And I am not

The gulf is wide for now
You throw fits and cry
Sometime ignoring all
The rules of proper

That's all right
You go ahead and do it
We know the situation
Far more is in your brain
Than you can say
Out loud except to shout
Your boy sweat and sweetness
Punctuated by the fullness
Of your laughter, of your kisses
Of your tears

I, for one, do understand
In adulthood, I'm silenced
Envy you your time to play
I have none left with candle
Burned fully at both ends
Save your time of excess
Until you need it most
Like when you're sixteen
For now know this one thing:
Sometimes a little crazy
    is a state of mind we share

Medical Destiny

Somewhere between the dreams and destiny
You found your way to medicine and miracles
Now looking back, measuring the force of it
A testament to your mettle, to your iron will

First to say it could be done and then to do it
Celebrated talent drawn up to persevere
Late nights, brain-pounding, hard-line tests,
One more lecture just beyond your sanity
Close that book and open up the next

Future promises fat with your wisdom now:
Salvation to the mother of a fevered child
Swift decisions made firm and sure
Blood and vessels cauterized

Bad news when it comes to knock
Delivered with your special care
The light of love, your best gift,
Fully given to this, your calling

Ready now to heal the sick
Offering all you do, full liberties
To fate or God or spirit master
You'll decide and do it

Damn the Norwegians

Every single time I leave
Those damned Norwegians come
Descending like a tribe of black spiders
They drop in from the spider sky
And cover you with kisses and their velvet legs
No doubt about it, they do it all
Cook hearty dishes, sweep the floor
One efficient gang, slaving long and hard
So effective and efficient in the kitchen
They mix drinks, bake bread, butter biscuits
As you sit like the king of the castle glowing
In their limelight while they waltz around
On their hateful spider legs
Anticipating all you ever need
Norwegian niceness, sticky sweet
So from the land of ice and snow
Those cold arachnids better watch it
I will be home
Coming from some distant shore
They best scatter in the wind
For if I found a spider in my bed
With sweet revenge, I'd weave a web
Taking murderous delight as
The black widow

Gaze from the Back Forty

Spring has come to the back forty
He sees her in the distance
Woman and horse are one
Galloping, their rhythms sync to
   heartbeats, to hooves on ground
"Golden" falls from his lips
Fair hair against black horse
He takes note – one woman, one horse
This blissful, mild spring day
Meant for napping, for bees buzzing
For newborn calves and fresh buds
An azure sky like the Mediterranean
Green pasture, a sea of native grasses
   Against a whisper of wind
Weather perfect, one cloud passing
Yellow sunflowers, heads grown heavy
Full, fat blue jays on the wing
The sun is mild, just at twelve o'clock
Some magic hour, he thinks
Sunrays on her hair like diadems
Noon, but he is no one
Only the hand, the help, nothing more
She never sees him standing there
Half-hidden in the wild plum thicket
Cowhand in love with the boss's wife
   in the spring, because it's spring
In the back forty

To the Fullest

I've thought of you these last few days
Longing to let go and know the space
Created in your ascension into absence
From those who loved you, all of them

You always danced to the light fanatical
Like an ornament of hand-blown glass
One pristine glimpse of verve and swerve
Now the moment all undone.
A sudden blink and slide to nothingness
and now the dream is memory

Again, to hold that one bright spark whatever
Charged the plugs. Raw energy and might.
Purple fur, with red hat, now black bikini
Cupid's hue and orange juice. Blue water.

Bath tub, all perfumed, grass green,
Summer sun, soup and dumplings, Christmas fire
Vodka, iced and luxuriant across our lips
All for one long, lovely life of bliss and love
That you lived to the fullest for us all

We Two, Us

Beyond the obvious

Genes, pool of essence

Colors of the elements

Iron, beyond the rain

Beyond the sun and the stars

We are connected in a binding

In a blindness beyond the molecules

Into narratives of history

Only dreams and mist

No one can measure us

In depths or meaning

Maybe angels or the spirit gods

No test tubes or science

Will know the trust

Reason distilled as we lean in

Our miracle born between us

Ask questions, validate, but grant no options

And know just this one thing:

I am you and you are me and we are one

We are the universe, a legacy forever

Of all there is to say and count alone.

Just for now we two, us

A Couple Observed in Winter

Fort Worth in February winter cold
Ice in the air, on their breath
Long expanse of gray Trinity River
This, a cold beyond the grave
Elizabethan ice faire cold
With city slickers unaware
So cold blood freezes; winter birds
      Nailed to the spot
Prayers issued up to ice masters
All to no avail in the winter white

There is a bench and they are there
He is fire and heat imagined
She has been invisible
Loved, but unattended, untouched
Now quietly ignited
On fire, in his love
Flaming proof against the cold gray

Understanding nothing, she is his saint
His perfect lips, full and ripe
His long, dark hair cascades
Bedroom eyes an afterthought
Against his French accent
An interloper, I hear him say, "I love…"

Full and large in the space of things

This is one nice fantasy, temperatures
Rising, then falling, then rising again
Until hot steams its full measure
And they are on fire, together
One, measured in this dream against
Trinity River ice and my cold reality
As I walk on by

Of an Island Sicily

One blissful afternoon
We sipped sweet red wine
Opening our souls to Sicily
Under an azure sky, sea blue
Ancient depths
Subterranean Phoenicians
Their art all around us
In every measured breath
Both theirs and ours

We drank in all things Sicilian
Marsala churches, old men on motorbikes
Gleaming fish in markets, jazz at 2:00 a.m
Hotels crisply served with rose rooms
Old stone floors warm
With whispered grief and love

We tethered to our Texas roots
But gave way easily to Sicilian charms
To fresh squeezed oranges, wicked sweets
All before the dawn of real sobriety
At times when dreams dispelled
We walked with all those mountain ghosts
Through fog well-forged in narrow streets

All in a day's work
We met the mayor and Michelangelo

Stopping for ricotta cheese and honey
Safari travels to faraway away
Magic made in painted tiles and olive oil
Midnight light through silver lemon trees
Guided to our silent prayers and on

We visited a villa, party in full swing
Pizza oven-fired we were invited
To dance and find the beat in centuries
Long gone before us in the cadence
Smiles, both theirs and ours
Spoke every bay-leafed syllable
Translated friendship without
A common language in the mix

Praise old-templed gods for calling us
We were of an island for a time
Knew the kin within our bones
Felt the sea and smelled the salt
Tasted all that came to us
All of it in Sicily, Sicily, Sicily

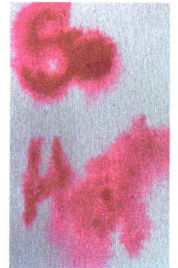

That Other Name

The long line snakes down the street, past
        A.F. Weaver's studio, almost to Rexall Drug.
Lila Stone, her long blond hair made picture perfect,
        Loves boys and kisses them
Frequently in the balcony of the Grand
Grand with a capital G, movie theatre
Other places too and just as well
Mineral Wells girls have a way of being hot
Right there, no shadow cast by the Baker Hotel.
So when Elvis's movie comes to town
They flock for a ticket like so many geese
Gaggling, they line up, joyful
All for loving the King of Rock 'n Roll

Shoving her money through the window,
Lila smiles and sweetly drawls
        "I'll have one ticket, mister."
The movie "Easy Come, Easy Go" features
Nine new songs, anthems all
        of Lila's personal love life.

Lila takes a seat by handsome Carl Ezel,
Football star who's never noticed her at school
When lights go dim, he takes her hand
        and shoulders up a bit.
Then Elvis launches into song,
And Lila is in love.

"Elvis, oh Elvis," she breathes
So heavily and hot her glasses fog
Cloud of unknowing descending
Lila takes Carl's hand and puts it to her breast
Awed by this miracle, he leans in for a wet kiss
Lips touch, but Lila is shipboard with Elvis
In deep B Flat right into that kiss.

When the movie ends, Elvis and the movie girl live
        happily ever after, but Lila knows the truth.
Elvis belongs to her, not some celluloid chick.
Carl never seems to mind that she calls him by
        that other name.

Your Poem

"After a person dies, the score evens up."

That's exactly what you said

As though you were the Dali Lama

Pondering from his mountain top

Or perhaps the Pope giving audience

What did you mean? Please be precise

I'm not dead yet,

And I don't have a scorecard.

Advice at Twenty-five

Landmark quarter-century

French class, no Paris

Summer drudgery before you walk

Graduation marks a moment

Across the stage, at last

Big on your mind and mine

But certainly not the main thing

Watching you become

Knowing you're a good man

True to yourself, true to your talent

Marching to a distant cadence

Not quite defined just yet

But that's ok since you know

Left foot from the right.

I taught you that and how to notice

Phrases too long before the verb

Shakespeare on the page

Bad poetry, good film

Rich chocolate, fine silk

How to set a table, how to say

"This is he," instead of "him"

Finish what you start and

Don't do guilt or lie

Love your family

Some excess is fine without excuse

Drive well and pay attention

No points for old ladies on the crosswalk

Know British comedy is best
As are the Beatles
This recap, life's wisdom freely given
All from me to you
Now that you're a quarter century

Lyrical Hope

They've seen it all—war and famine, plague, spontaneous combustion.
They've kept him safe and taught him by the book
How to hope, live the Golden Rule, compete.
For this chaotic world, he needs the necessary tools:
Wit and charm, vocabulary, cinematic knowledge
Know good chocolate and how to braise a roast.

They've noticed that he's special, and tried to tell him so.
A child beyond his years, an old soul whose universal tuning fork
Radiates across the miles and to the moon and back.
Music courses through his veins, so he's protected.
Full intent to play his passion, write the masterpiece
Knowing all the notes does help, but if he sometimes fails to
      hear the tune, it will be all right.
He'll find the beat.
He'll see the inspiration in the light and go there.
They know he'll find the best metaphor,
And sing his song in perfect harmony.

Across the years he's made them proud to be his parents.
They've heard the horror stories.
Angst-ridden, tattooed and tortured
      lost boys who never find their way.
But he has perfect pitch and plays so well.
Thank God, his symphony has never disappointed.

So they tell him, mark this time and listen for the future beat.
His cadence so inspiring, so promising, so full of possibilities
He will go forth and be the music in a major chord.
Dance, one and all

Let's Suppose You Know

Let's suppose you know
That I look into the deep pools of your eyes
And I see Africa. Sun deep in red sand. Hot.
You, longing for ebony, for history, for her history
But you pass by, longing still in the moonlight
Listening to lions pass in the bush. Knowing them
In their full flavor, a danger so complete you
Know sublime and close your eyes against
The siren call. In your tent on the savannah
Alone, the die cast for your fate without her.

Let's suppose you know
That in my dreams you call to me
Walking in the sand, you stop and smell the surf
Take count of boats on far horizon. The day is
Full of promise. Cloudless azure sky in full color.
Murmurs on the breeze. French phrases in the air.
Our cottage perched on a precipice full view
Napoleon's ramparts of a time, relentless waves
I watch you walking up the path through bougainvillea
Framed in pink blossoms, rich like spun sugar
Coming in our doorway, you bring the mystic
Mist. Sage. Lavender. A hint of musk.
You take my hand and kiss it
Gently, your breath against my skin
This is like Virginia's drowning
Without the rocks in pockets
Without the lovely water

Tupelo, Oh Tupelo

Memphis natives told us not to make the drive

Forget the traffic, plenty to see right here

We'd had enough of Graceland's glitter

So we headed east to find the history

Elvis's birthright all the family

A two-room house built by his father

A no-good guy we learned, who womanized

Forged a four dollar check for forty

All for the price of a pig he'd sold

Vernon, descendent of a rogue sister

One who never married, but had sons

A legacy of ne'er do wells until the one child

He could sing, came in cute and happy

Age three warbling in the church

With varnished pews and resonating walls

Perfect for a small voice, so angelic sweet

That people held their breath

His mama encouraging from the front row

He scratched his knee, then belted out

A Jesus song knowing well her favor

He pleased her as he should

To have the promised sweets

He could taste them now

Bowl overflowing on the kitchen table

In the back room by the fire, golden warm

Pentacostal, devout to gospel chords

Then they pause, paying homage

To the future music, all to rock n'roll
A glimpse back then of what would be
Sun Studios, blockbuster record spins
Money gold, so much it lit the sky
So many toys appeared in his Memphis yard
The jeeps and snowmobiles, not to mention
Guns and TV sets, more to shoot and watch
He left Tupelo, but in his wake they celebrate
All of it, all that fame and glamour
His distant cousin in the gift shop
A schoolmate just younger, same teacher
Giving tours. We're closer than the six degrees
We feel it in the trees, on the steps of Milam Middle School
Elvis's last Tupelo moments with his friends
Boys who knew him well, girls who knew his touch
Elvis lived here and loved it all
Moved on, but always dreamed and whispered
Tupelo, oh Tupelo in his sleep

A Million Miracles

I believe in Wordsworth's transcendental love
And promise for our DNA carried future-wise
You have your ticket, held tightly while you bide your time
Among the cosmic points of light, watching us
Watching us waiting while biology sets the magic note
To sound in nine round months, awakening to the music
Our music so lingering and lovely in its contrapuntal cadence
Our family song to fill us up and make us pure.
Beyond ourselves to know this miracle as cells divide
And we stand back to wait while nature and the universe align.

A prayer, a thought, and into being with the dance
You'll jump feet first, move right then left to shift the source
If this is your time, and we cannot know for sure, so be it.
I am here to welcome you, my sweet pea who will someday
Pat my hand, believe me beautiful, and always know
celestial light and bliss in all your baby sweetness.

So now I wait, not daring to presume the singleness
Of this great, good plan, the pieces of its passing
The journey of a million miracles now beginning
To take us to the full moon of your birth and our life's legacy

Winning Ticket

She will give him all of it, all she has
Make a happy life, offer herself up
Until her chrysalis can never bloom
Passion overtaking, and she a dry husk
All for his demons to dispel
All knotted up against his hard core
Stomach muscles, blood, hot heat
Too much defended by 1-2-3
Of his routine, of dirt, or former wars
Of hard drugs in veins, of sweat pooling

She hardly knows him when she looks at him
So filled with need, refusing all discovery
Heavy burden as he slides dollar bills
Lottery luck, this machine, these tickets
Into the slot, hoping for a better life

One that he imagines with cigarettes
And porn stars, all in limbo against the grain
Momentary relief against his pain
Who is she to say what satisfies
Because he can't know for sure

He has had more women than she can count
All of them beautiful and sleek beyond her
Unsatisfied against the possibilities
Perverse in pleasure of her pain

They did not lift his heaviness
His soul so burdened by consequence
Of a failed marriage and lost son
Of a dead father whose success was drained
Of a mother oblivious to his pain
Of sisters who know nothing and care less

He needs her, more than ever now
In this moment, refusing all the signs
The vision when it comes, the darkness waxing
She is his angelic hope, finally the tie that binds
Impossible for him to live without her

Kiss her now. You have a winning ticket.

Part II

For Dylan: On the Demise of a Very Good Cat

1

I'll light a candle for you
I'll light it for nine long days
Reaching to your nine cat spirit lives
Grateful that you spent one with me

2

Your glowing eyes spelled mystic, finely born
Gray white-thick fur quaked as your motor ran

3

You knew what you liked, what you didn't
Never one to mince feelings or fangs

4

Once you ordained the bathmat
My lover's soggy footprint, foreign fear
He begged to make you disappear, but no luck

5

Biggest cat in Erath County the vet had said
I kept your food dish full, an act of necessity

6

Performing better than Marcel Marceau
One, two, three I'd say, toss treat into the air

You, poised and ready, then reaching hard
Lightening paw grabbing and then you have it
Delivered morsel into your pink mouth

                    7

We always said you should be on TV.

                    8

And you would have been, but for the *3 P's*
The kids were young, so I euphemized
We mopped up puke, piss, poop
       from the floorboard of the car
They knew the real truth

                    9

All in all I have to say I loved you. Simply that.
You loved me back.
And that's more than anyone should ask of a big gray cat.

Oasis Love

Save thankless, squalling, parasitic kids
She'd long since ceased to love
Nothing, no thing left for her
Domesticity sucked her dry with
Too much laundry and dirty dishes in the sink

Her husband was no help
He gave it all to smooth women and their cars
Crushed fenders, off-beat gages
And to men with stoked transmissions
Swearing strong, oil pressure strength
Talking fast, cars and carburetor candy

She had given all she had, and so had he at first
Until the husk that he dragged home
Was something she could hardly recognize

Nothing, no thing left for her
She tried to laugh it off, act like a socialite
Smiled, talked on deaf ears, summer steady
Shared in one-way streets and empty alleys

One day, she'd had her fill.
Hands on hips, she looks into his dead eyes
Takes a breath and a leap and says:
"Tell you what I'm going to do
Now that you're sucked dry,

Distilled for that almighty dollar
I'm looking for oasis love.
Misty, moist, in full bloom
Can you feel it?
I've just licked my liquid lips."

Just There

She could be his lover, his love
A tall man from Brooklyn
Ever ready, ever dark in circumstance
Her look becomes a siren call.

Listing and listening, she sees him.
She comes into his space.
Reluctantly at first, knowing nothing
These circumstances tell her little
But later she will know

A hotel room miles away from things familiar
A neon light she's never seen before
Radio on low tones with little to discern
Her soft sweater there against her neck
His wet wool coat, oh, so heavy now
She smells it, broadcast molecules

He has been distant until now
Until blood runs hot
Until breath turns to vapor
Until sweat runs down the nape
Until clothes pile at their feet
And her hand feels the wet cold smoothness

In the shower, her stare, glassy-eyed
She looks at her hand, splayed against the glass
Delphi's oracle. Just there. Just there.
She knows her needs and he fulfills them

Just there. Just there.

Father-Daughter Observed

He is her father all be told, and wise
By force of years and longing
By time counted in degrees
In courses, in essays, in committees
He has a PhD and knows to measure
He knows the metrics and the field
He knows the particles waving
He is the universe defined

He has led a life so fully satisfied
With studied countenance and reserve
British manners curt, sophisticated
Gentleman's code apparent
In pin-striped suit, Italian shoes
Black hair graying at the temples
He's an Esquire ad with more finesse

And here's the girl, all but insignificant
He is Zeus, but she is not Athena
A small flash across the starry sky
A moment way beyond his depth
He sums her up dismissing
Her attempts to care and hold

Spiky blond-haired babe
Cute, but not so pretty, sassy
Leather skirted, waif-like

Too trendy for her own good
Steel blue eyes piercing
Under heavy, green-shadowed lids
She's a Hollywood Tim Burton
Silver-screened imagining all awry
Uncomfortable as a misplaced modifier

She reaches out, takes his hand
But he will have none of it
Surveys the scene, begs leave
Reaches into his beast pocket
Extracts that black credit card
In a hurry now, hands it over
Turns and disappears fast
Blink and gone, gone, gone

She tallies up the circumstance
Wiser by the force, by the reckoning
By experience, by the long of it
By all those childhood disappointments
Observing, now alone in the crowd
No grace given from the father
Ruler of the cosmos, slayer of her heart
That's fine says her Mona Lisa smile

She's off to fill the hole, off to shop

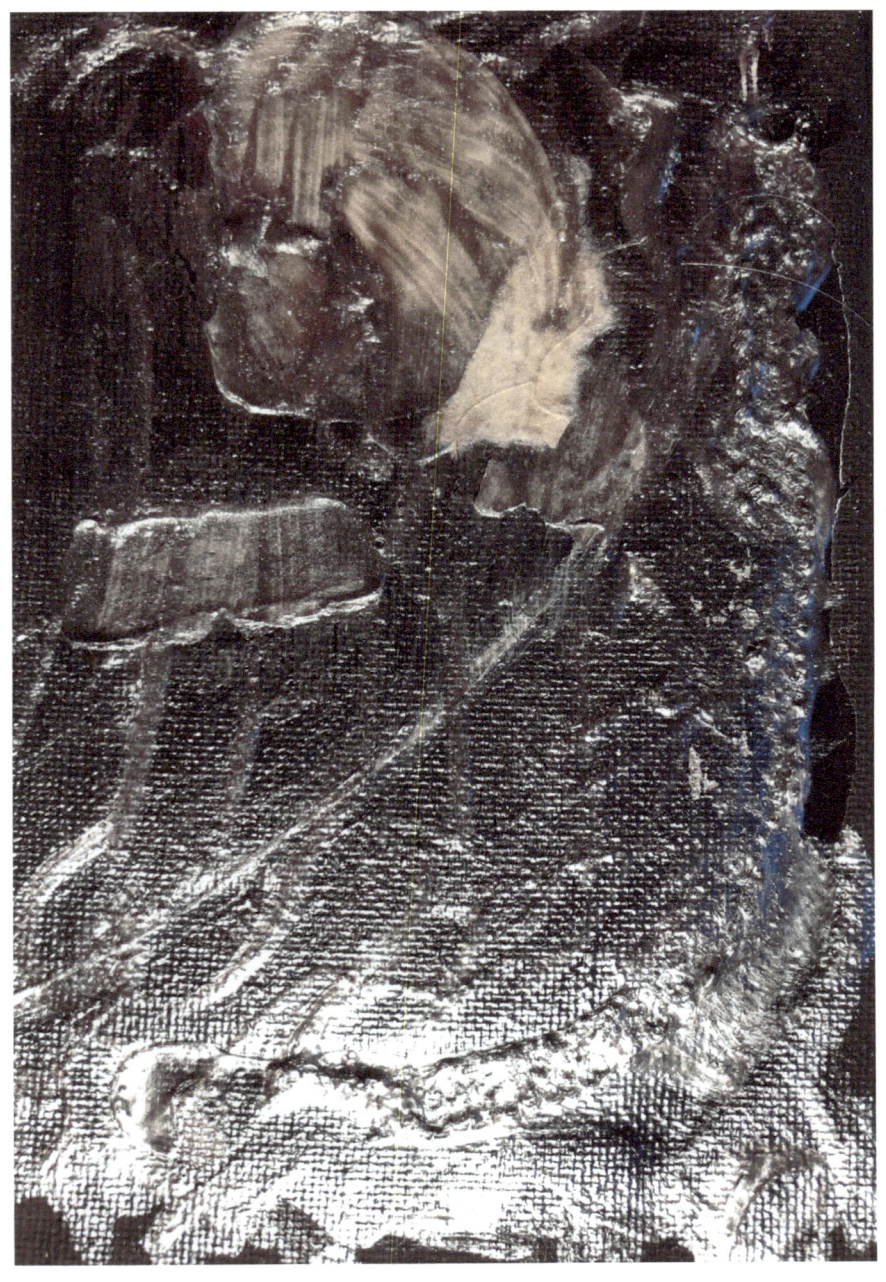

Starlight in Guadalajara

We danced and drank tequila hard

Sweet, lime-breath until we couldn't stand

But held on tight in the Mexican starlight

In Guadalajara where everybody has secrets

We inhaled the view and each other

Holding dear promises and an anniversary

I don't remember which, maybe tenth

Maybe more, but all the same satisfaction

Mexico has secrets, as do we now

From knowing all we know about each other

We leave things, all the best unsaid

The night is dark and dancing full of music

Rich in love and pink

Flowers blooming, heavy scents like burnt sugar

I don't know how to take it in

Except to say it:

This is Guadalajara

Where there are no rules,

Him, me, love,

And then a falling star

Obscure Blessings

It's late summer afternoon in Austin
Sixth Street landscape in the cool
Driskill Hotel Bar where secrets
Hold against dark wood, against time

He is a bright delight to behold
A man defined by long hair, dark eyes
Dancing, ever intriguing and beguiling
Against the absurd backdrop of her love

Older by decades, Liz Taylor heyday
Bejeweled for the red carpet
In a little black dress from Neimans
Nursing him and a tropical drink

In the 60s she wooed a velvet Elvis
Now she's discovered something else
Just as rich, more lip-quenching
Time-defined wrinkles not lost on him

She offers a plump strawberry overripe
Thrust by design into his luscious mouth
Juice dripping, streaming down his chin
Fantasy-sweet like goblins in the market

He waltzes through this landscape
His hold on her so perfectly explicit
Offering nothing, the god of reticence
Defined by her and circumstance

His look leaves questioning to lesser mortals
No bother with her fantasies or theirs
His talent for disdain obscures the blessing
Hers to look beyond it, taken in by youth

He will heed her many desperate favors
With his smooth body and quick breath
By her need and gratitude and love
By her money

The Wise Woman of the Rock

You give us ebb and flow of life, green sea
and red sky and turtle wisdom
You breathe metal strength, hammered
White hot against Sedona sun
We know and we are, time immortal
All and best we ride against the tide
Of time, all love but fear to be
Wise Woman of the Rock
You give us all there is to know and then some
We incandescent bear the load and come with hope
One on one, then parting comes so sweet
And all too brief from this world to the next
Death and travel all alone until we're met by the
Wise Woman of the Rock

   Loving purples, red, blue, and greens
   Against the sunset sky. A gift to satisfy the thirst
   For drinking in the elements returned to dust
   Artful characters dance the dance and we are there.

   Mystic Mesa meets the moment and we commune
   Three humans with the cosmos all adrift in sync
   The red, red rock and that one Woman of the Rock
   You take us by the hand, then sing us to the force

   The Wise Woman of the Rock in all directions
   Winds from north, south, east, and west.

She guides us, satisfied to know the truth.
Smoke the pipe of peace, walk the medicine wheel,
Grant the gifts through her ordained.

The Wise Woman of the Rock says it clear:
Blessed be the moment now all inspired
Dance the dance, sing the song
Now and forever afterwards
In the red, red rock

The Expatriates

Swimming in perfect grief or some unsustainable truth
I hear it in their voices — a certain summer sadness
They tell of other lives they've lived, not why they left
I wonder at their easy sacrifices
They chose an Italian future over an American dream
Always a divorce or some high crime or missed connection
With round-trip tickets they'll never need again
They make their art here courting finer muses
Old lives give way to new and all agree
That it takes time to reinvent a life

They learn the language to a luminous perfection
That leaves me speechless
Uncluttered, acculturated, they blend in so well
Looking home-grown in the Tuscan hills
Looking homeward

Tribal Love

Welcome to the tribe, Baby

Youngest member of the band, the clan, your family

Bound by blood and DNA, connections inescapable

Never, ever doubt the bone of our bond

The depth of love from all of us

And we have no agenda, no single thing to go on

We hardly know you or your ways, and yet you have it all:

Our faith in you and who you will become to do us proud

Strong and gallant, polite we hope and promising

Even in your babyhood, a sweetness light and charming

Full-forced and handsome in your teens

A man well educated and kind to animals and the elderly

Crossin Clark Griggs

With a unique name brought all the way from Ireland

By a great-great grandmother who crossed an ocean to New York City

All the way from Belfast, escaping God knows what in her flight

Catherine Isabell Crossin

Would be glad to know her surname hangs on you like a medal

Bright and bold and beautiful

You'll make your way and stay the course

Tribal knowledge leading you to good decisions

Fine strong values and strength of character

Supported by a brother, pampered by two sisters

Your mother tends to you and to the sick

Your father's creativity flows through your veins

Somewhere, someday you will gaze eastward across the sea

Breathe deep, and wonder at your thoughts of Ireland

Or perhaps marvel when you dream of bonny Scotland
Marshaling the Griggs's great highland spirits
We, and all our unassailable Gaelic ancestors, welcome you
Steeled to the hilt for all good things in this life
Now go and live it, and be mindful, full of gratitude
For tribal love

Birth

I remember thirty years ago today
Blooming into the world
You jumped in feet first
Announced in no ways regular
You slept soundly that fall morning
Oblivious that the time had come
Then poked and prodded, told to look outside
You moved first one way, then the next
Stretching, fist against the ceiling, knee in my rib
Then whoosh and there you were
Pulled out through a healthy passageway
A nice, wide exit right across my belly
Blinking in the light, red faced, but perfect
Head round and beautiful
Not like those other babies we saw
With pointed pates like Coneheads
Saturday Night Live infant-style
Fresh and happy, unencumbered
Unblemished by a squeeze through a canal
Something to be said for a baby who comes with no labor
Whose mother has a good night's sleep, then checks in
Smiling amid the scrubbed nurses and one doc
His last words to me had something
To do with counting backwards from ten
I got to nine before the stars were shining
      on some distant shore
Then there you were, a surprise package
A gift to us on your birthday.

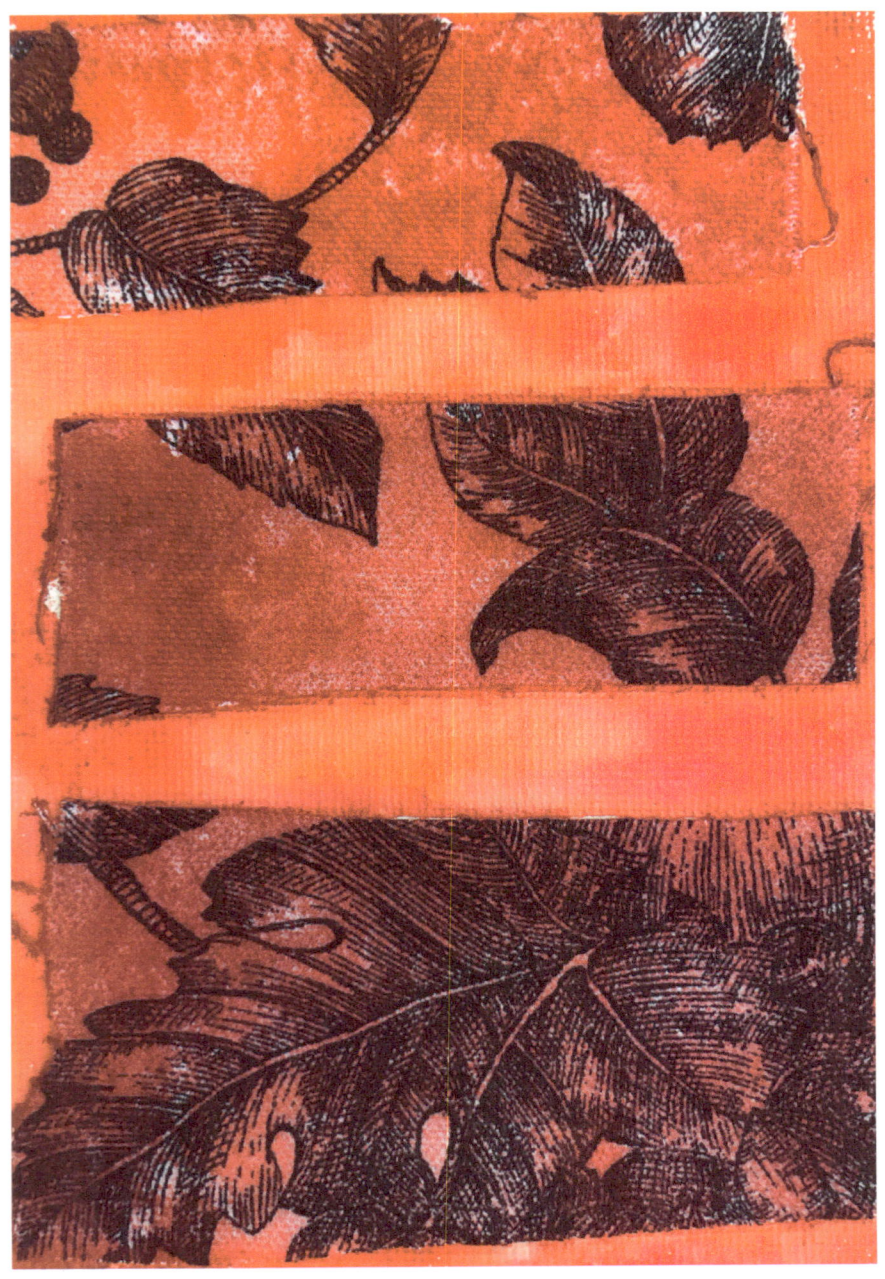

Fair Fever

We have Fair Fever in the fall
Orange leaves and pumpkin spice
We note the good October air
Crisp with hints of what's to come
North winds gathering, but no ice yet
Traditions pass through generations
Dallas high life in October
Returning to my birthplace
Drawn there on my birthday
By forces working bold magic
Then we buy those tickets
State Fair of Texas
Crime or parking problems
Don't deter us from our pilgrimage
Practice the religion of all things fried
Beer and butter, pickles and prickly pears
Big Tex is priest, protector of unruly flocks
We gawk and laugh, astounded by the sights
That dancing chicken, Elvis on stilts
Blue ribbon on a blue-eyed doll
World exotica to buy, a showroom full of cars
The Midway, a kind of purgatory on the way
    to corn dog heaven
Temperatures drop, but fever rises
It is the fall, lovely fall
It is with me in my October light
   and in my children
   and in my children's children
Thanks be
We won't be cured.

Real Action

Her cousin's room was teen-heaven
Smelled like Este Lauder Youth Dew drenching
Smooth, white skin radiant and moist in promises
The day was lazy and so long, as they all
      sprawled across the pink petal bedspread
Leafed through fan magazines and popped their gum
      Talked about bad boys and heavy petting.

The girl was nine, primped and primed
There by special invitation
Usually, they slammed the door,
Told her to go outside, go away
Play with screaming neighbor kids
Who in the grime and muck of games
Like lunatic red rover never called her name.
It made her cross and mean to think of it

Today was different since they had asked her in
Hangin' with the big girls who knew how to flirt
Take long bubble baths, stuff their bras.
She wore her rhinestone cat-eye sunglasses
Even inside, especially inside to be cool
Sitting oh-so-still and calm, while they painted her toenails
      With cherry-hot kissable fire engine red polish.

Elvis was their man, the crooner in the backdrop
Always the only voice in the stack of 45s

The stereo in the corner, an altar to the King.
The big girls had female fantasies, so when he sang
Love me tender they closed the book
And each one, on her own, had her way with him.
Growing limp and damp, the cousin dream-kissed
    her Elvis, bold while he sang her name.

The girl had missed the moment by a good five years.
So she was bored with all their starry-eyed silliness
Jumped down off the bed to slice a hole right through
    the silken tent of sex and glamour.
"You're stupid Elvis-heads," she shouted.

Knocked against the record player and the King's
    velvet voice jerked into a scratchy bleat
She exited quick, took her red toenails and sunglasses
    outside to scout for real boys, real action.

Because she was nine, now primped and primed
Tender love only dreamed, Elvis be damned.
Some real boy would call her name
And she would kiss him.

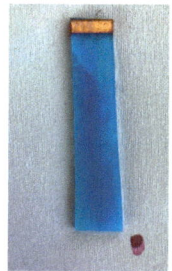

Sunlit on the Beach at St. Tropez

Eighty if day, she's sure this is perfection found
This afternoon so *paradiso* that she remembers 1942
When she made sure the soldiers in her village
Knew her name, knew the bread she made
Brown and crusty hot, served with dark red wine
Remembered them and their good looks
Always the nice girl, she kept her distance
As American boys marched through
Young and uncertain, all eager for experience

She throws her blue blanket onto the sand
Surmising the view, deep across the water
Across the Mediterranean azure and smooth
A slight wind blows, and she sees birds take flight
Sun hot on white sand, bright, high in the sky
A boy comes by offering a chaise, a stripped umbrella
But she says no and thank you. *Merci.*
She likes the hard, steady feel of sand beneath her
No feeble-minded thoughts, only clarity

She lies down to feel the warmth, the sureness
Thinking of those boys in uniform
Like every other woman on the beach that day
She disengages first one strap and then the other
Revealing fine white breasts like porcelain
Unblemished by the years, untouched of late
Nipples like roses blossoming and sweet

Reckoning the heft, she lies down to sleep
Soon to dream, bare-breasted
Of those boys in uniform, one in particular
Of lazy afternoons when bees buzzed loud
When sirens warned of Germans
And one young dimpled man who smiled
Secrets she would never know until this day
When sunlit thoughts had their way with her

One

One big boy
One sky
One blue
One cool sheet
One soft breeze
One lip lock
One lazy
One long breath
One nap
One boy dream
One stretch
One big scream
One warm push
One birthday
One cake
One light beam
One cosmos
One family
One big love
Yours truly
One year old

Spaces in a Connecticut Road

Savor the moment in the cool green

Valley of forgetfulness all in full

A rich scent of verdant luminescence

in a sliver of haze across the way

Air heavy and blue, slightly damp

Clinging to my forgetfulness

You and me and a silver Corvette

Warm hood against our bodies

Against our backs in the sun now

We do inhale and breathe the deep

Allure of youth and time

It's still. It's quiet. It's ours.

Then we see a mouse painted sure

In landscape just in front of the

Shark-like car, the nose pointing

It's there, and we commune

Awestruck, incredulous—a mouse

Then suddenly, in cosmic tragedy

A hawk swoops in to take its prey

And we are left with nothing

Little, less, then none

Only our warm bodies against the

Cool metal of the shark-like car

We kiss to know that we are real

Of a Moment Wild

Port Aransas beach where the living was not so easy
Washed out jeans and old cars, too much beer and
No satisfaction for the trouble
We found our way there with an ice chest and wild ones
Too untamed to notice that we had class and a dark blue Superbee
Cool and lots of horsepower under our hood, bolted up against
Stoned hooligans, one word mine, one word my mother's
Who thought we were on a mission trip to save sad souls.

We were, I guess, but not to pray or lead the youth away from sin
We were inequities blessed with good highs and a fast car and funds
We booked a room in a hotel dump, forego the tent and sand fleas
Life is hard, but for good kids gone bad, not so much
The hotel smelled like dull sweat, but we were of the moment
Knowing this was our time of sordid pleasure
Breathing in. Breathing out.
We paid the fee for that twenty-five cent mattress massage.

Then we merged with the mob on Port Aransas beach.
We plumped the air mattress, lay among the bad boys, and drank beer
More beer than humans should consume under a summer sun on a
     hot beach
We were of a moment wild, gone all bad to a dark place
Where love was on the radio, and we kissed long and hard
Bleached from sun, we slept like dead beached whales
All encompassed by the waves, by the bad boys, by the beer.

I awakened to the end of the world, hot flames bearing down
Swollen brain, heavy, dull-lidded and befuddled, one lost soul
Crawl on hands and knees in forced supplication to the toilet god
And wish that I was dead, skin red and burning.
Where, I wondered, was the glamour?

Ethiopian Friend

This is a selfish thing, I know to try to measure one time
One time in the great good beat of history that never ends
The great good beat that lets us know we are connected
Tied at the life's blood core of human beats and hearts
Those who know of sun and dirt and rain and all of it
Those whose hope is iron strong for more, for trust
For trust in the great promise, by our great promise
Knowing wise that potential lies in partnership, a show
That somehow we connect at hearts' blood to feel the beat
The will to give a name to mutual trust; the will to work it all.

Ethiopia, we hold you common brothers. All of it around us.
Charged heat of summer, cattle grazing, water on the wane
Strong, dark coffee, country brush, charmed circles interlocked
The famine has been won, now life betides the fruit of it
Sure that all we work has found the fullness and the use

Strong connections, bold for better future bright for both of us
For water glimmering in the lakes, we'll pray for rain together
In knowing how to measure, how to build the chance
Find some poetry, dance some magic, play the drums
Enchant the testing strengths for sureness in the water's flow

Please know that in the depth and heft of all things golden
I thank you for this friendship made,
Texas, Ethiopia, cultures bound together now for good
Going home, remember me, this night, and keep best memories
Best kept when keeping full, when the full moon rises
Look in this direction, and wave to me. I'll do the same.

Virgin

I have lived the life of the good girl
Honor society, Church of Christ,
Holding my knees together
No beer, no smokes, no stolen kisses
I am good beyond endurance
Beyond hormones raging
Beyond peer pressure and easy drugs
My bedroom door swings to an outside porch
But I don't leave in the moonlight when
Jeff, the bad boy, beckons. I say no.
No, flits off my lips in measured tones
And he dies of desire and wantonness
No to tight skirts and too much jewelry
No to late nights and cigarettes
No to blue eye shadow on heavy lids
I steel myself for worse temptations
And then it comes.
He is exotic with dark, bedroom eyes.
He is Catholic and doesn't care
He's from New Jersey, a foreign land
That I don't know or understand
His smoothness silver and miraculous
As are his kisses, and then before I know it
We are there.
On my grandmother's quilt
Under the trees. Under the stars. Alone.
Drinking in each other and my innocence
Is gone

Prunes

Surrounded by idiots in candy-stripe
They smile like weasels
She knows better now, knows it all
They hate the time and clocks
Hate her wicked eye that tracks them
In the day room the smell is peppermint
An odor she has always hated
Especially mixed with chocolate
Candies for the weak-minded;
For the infirm; for the stupid
They force feed them on Thursdays
When the Church of Christ come calling
Blue-haired women in double-knit
Pandering honey-tongued men
She has long since passed desire
Passed the pleasures of the flesh
And God and Bible dribble
Moved on to sky lovers who come
In dreams despite the smell of urine.
She gives it all to them and to angelic sex.
And steels herself against inanities
She calls for prunes to share when
Her one relative comes calling
A groveling niece who wants one thing:
The jewelry in her bank vault
"Have a prune," she shouts at her.
Scared rabbit of a girl, slight and small

Probably never had a prune, partial to those
Plump, purple plums, so she declines
All polite and sniveling, "Oh, no, thank you."
Before the girl can coo again, the old woman gathers it
Shouts again, "I said for you to eat a goddamn prune."
Again, the girl refuses, sliding into tears.
Prunes go helter-skelter, making ugly tracks
Down white-washed walls, shit-colored ribbons
You're a stupid girlie thinks the ancient one.
And then she shouts "So constipate and die."

45th Anniversary

I see you now in my mind's eye

Nineteen and very New York

Exotic in taste and texture

Dark eyes, black hair, Catholic

The fire ignited bright and hot

Under the stars in dew and kisses

How did we make this life

Unknowing in our bliss and blessed

Together in a universe of cars and books

One garage apartment on Lillian

With a silver Vette in the driveway

As unlikely a car as a Rolls

For two broke college kids

Finances all along the lines of zero

With tuition, bills, and rent

We summered in New England

Like rich people glamorized

Friends toiled and studied hard at home

While we two played hard and fast

Flitting through towns and backwaters

Beer in the cooler, smoke in the ashtray

Wanderlust spilling on the highways

We were good kids who set no limits

Driving deep into America

With each other and our dreams

There it is. There it is.

Therein lies the secret of 45 together

Wild and crazy, we never grew apart
We underscored the drama
Through blue skies and summer days
Your business savvy, my determination
We are who we have become
Together, not like normal folk,
Ever-ready to experiment
Force the luck, keen the edge
We have trekked fate's lunar landscapes
Believing we're a couple charmed
Your cows and green and tractors
My films and poetry
We might look a lot like opposites
But that is not the case
I am your best self and you are mine
Knowing now and sure a thing
As I knew then once upon a time

Epithalamium

Remember the bliss of this day as you go about your lives
The tally of it all in every shade of imaged pleasure
Breathe back perfected sea of Wordsworth's green
Mustang sally blue, unbridled white, elegance of black
Truth and detail in iridescent beauty silvered sleek

Take in the musical circumference and note the fine edge
Melodious message sung, text on wind sent straight to angels
Genius and talent brought together in one big bouquet
Of major and minor chords all glimmering
All tuned by the musician's perfect ear

Revisit each and every richness bestowed to you today
A child's small hand, a velvet petal in honeyed hue
Engaged senses to taste the wine and that one special kiss
The prayers, the vows, the shade and stand of light
All passing memories dedicated and delighted

Entwined in rapturous well-springs of good wishes
Brought to bear from friends and family who came
Tears of joy and life-blood of the covenant running deep
Shared arrangements come from goodness focused
Straight from their hearts into yours, the strongest power

Recollect the ghosts of ancestors among us
Those who wouldn't miss a wedding for the world
Fanned out in their infinitesimal authority
They're watching now from every vantage point

Destinies beyond death that have a way of proving love
Moment by moment wrapped in your heart's happiness
To take out one by one by one in good times and in bad
Life is never what the doctor ordered for contentment
Be prepared when silly things outpace family plans
And chance or tedium ruin weekly movie nights

Life will be good to you blessed, beyond all measure
In God's all-perfect circle because love comes from God
Moments recollected in tranquil times will be sweetest
Freshly born in new radiance as two together become one
Know all you need is love and knowing you are loved

Strawberries and Smooth Jazz

He is a delight to behold
A man defined by long hair and dark eyes
Dancing, ever intriguing and beguiling
Against a black backdrop of her imagination

She wants smooth, silky, lazy strains of jazz
Something harmonizing rich
Something sweet, lip-quenching
Oh, that sax

Let's go with strawberries ripe
Dripping down their chins
On a summer afternoon in Dallas
McKinney Avenue at the Ritz

Nothing reality defined, only fantasy
As he waltzes through the landscape, and she takes note
He has a hold on women that cannot be explained
They line up, take him in, and ask for more

He never offers himself up
He is the god defined of reticence
Of waiting until later for the right time
Of asking circumstance, weighing it
Of needing to know more, more

He leaves the questioning to lesser mortals

He cannot be bothered with her fantasy
She smiles and prays he'll make a move
Taken in by him, to be taken by him

By his movie star good looks
By his talent to please
By his smooth body and sweet breath
By his heft and her need
By him
But he walks on by with no promise
        Of strawberries or smooth jazz

For my Aunt Flossie (Winona) and Summer, 1957

Your light burned hard and long, Winona Bowen.
You pushed through poverty and pain to
      make us sweet, uneasy poetry
In stone-carved manuscripts. You always looked for more,
      the next best thing to take our breath away.

Of all the memories to keep, I like the first one best.
Still keen across time, the picture well-defined.
It was the summer of 1957.
Rabbit-ears adjusted on the black and white TV,
I ate Cheerios, watched Captain Kangaroo
Made mud-pies, played dolls, sang to August wind.
I was five years old, nearly six when you arrived.

In the haze of summer sun, I watched you
Tall, lean, and beautiful, sleek and promising silk
Arriving in a white Cadillac, you and your man
Waltzed right up our stone steps with a brand new baby.

Fresh in from the road, all the way from Phoenix
You smelled of some sweet scent I didn't know
You breezed in, lit up a cigarette, and sat that baby on a quilt
So I could get a better look up close.
You smiled at me, touched my hair, held my hand
And introduced my one and only cousin
Your one and only baby, perfumed from your presence.

You didn't stay the night, only one August afternoon
The visit punctuated with strong iced tea and sandwiches
Then hugs, kisses all around as we said our goodbyes.

I stood on the front porch, truly all amazed
by your coming to the country, to the farm
Your city radiance beaming glamour and glory
      like it was the second-coming, not the first.

In the final moments, brilliant Uncle Johnny
      your shining knight, pushed a magic button
And the hard top of that white Caddy
Unfolded, slowly into the trunk like it was Harry Houdini's,
Now you see it now you don't.
You laughed and flashed that Hollywood smile,
The light on your dark hair and rhinestone-studded glasses
Adding to the glow that lit us up
My cow and chicken, mud-pie life now forever changed
Because from here on out, I had hopes and dreams.
I had Aunt Flossie whose gifts gave me
      my one and only cousin and real-life drama,
Precious gifts that only you could give.

Betrayal

Like a black snake
Coiled in a letter box
Slithery and cold
Within the warm heart
Of too much love
Fangs and poison
Brought large
Into focus of white heat
Better to know now
When skin is tough
When sobriety scales the wall
In cold, crisp morning air
Reminder that you never know
What darkness may be lurking
Toads with serpents
Hidden there among pink roses
In lights as bright as Vegas
In history old as Cairo's streets
As wild as Texas cowboys
Into the night into the night
Unhinged and sad with warts
All things left unsaid
One brainless bastard left to bask
In hell, bad seed and cursed
Once upon a time
She loved him

Moonlight and A Movie

Who knew what drama might arrive that clear clean night
I heard you say party and a movie
Or did you say party *for* a movie
But I have little space to know and don't ask
Traveling on narrow roads through dusk and dirt
We're going to Casa Caponetti
One village farm on a high green hill
Where people have parties for movies, but I don't ask

We arrive, then round the circle of your friends
Conversations in Italian run smooth and liquid
I smile a lot and say *buona sera*, all that I can do
For the likes of Eleonora and Giovanni
On short notice unless a miracle strikes me dead
And I die with Italian on my lips

We eat sausages, olives, bread, drink wine
Kissed by the hilltop breezes and the stars
Both real and box office
When the screening starts we sit on bales of hay
Arranged for perfect viewing, the screen against
A movie scene of Tuscan hills and moonlit sky

Images bring back the medieval dead
Back to the town's great churches, *sanctum sanctori*
I sit next to the man who plays the bishop
Praying himself to stardom and grace, whichever comes first
In Tuscania, one can't be sure

About the Author

Marilyn Robitaille is a writer, editor, film critic, and English professor. She co-edits *The Langdon Review of the Arts in Texas* and co-hosts *Langdon Review* Weekend, a Texas arts and letters festival in Granbury, Texas. Her poetry has most recently appeared in several literary anthologies including *Her Texas: An Anthology of Texas Women Writers; Writing Texas;* and *Texas Weather: An Anthology of Poetry, Short fiction, and Nonfiction.* She writes a weekly film review for the *Stephenville Empire Tribune* and the *Glen Rose Reporter.* She is Associate Professor of English at Tarleton State University, Member of the Texas A & M University System where she serves as Director of International Programs. She earned her M.A. from the Bread Loaf School of English, Middlebury College and her Ph.D. from Texas Woman's University. She lives on a ranch in Stephenville, Texas, with her husband Charles, a dedicated poodle named Louis Vuitton, and a fierce cat named Versace.

Index

A

Advice at Twenty-five 51

B

Baby Lovely 11
Betrayal 143
Birth 99

C

Couple Observed in Winter, A 37

D

Damn the Norwegians 29

E

Epithalamium 131
Ethiopian Friend 119
Expatriates, The 93

F

Fair Fever 101
Father-Daughter 79
Fine Blue Stone, A 9
First Christmas 5
For Dylan: On the Demise of a Very Good Cat 69
For My Aunt Flossie 139
45th Anniversary 127
Frank Sinatra Sighting in New York City, A 17

G

Gaze from the Back Forty 31

I

In Grace and Love 21

J

Just There 77

L

Let's Suppose You Know 57
Little Crazy, A 25
Lyrical Hope 55

M

Medical Destiny 27
Million Miracles, A 63
Montrose in August 15
Moonlight and a Movie 145
Mustang in the Park 1970 3

O

Oasis Love 73
Obscure Blessings 85
Of an Island Sicily 41
Of a Moment Wild on Port Aransas Beach 115
One 111

P

Prunes 123

R

Real Action 103

S

September Birthday Wish For you, A 7
She Waits 13
Spaces in a Connecticut Road 113
Starlight in Guadalajara 83
Strawberries and Smooth Jazz 135
Sunlit On the Beach at St. Tropez ... 107

T

That Other Name 45
To the Fullest 33
Tribal Love 95
Tupelo, Oh Tupelo 59

V

Virgin 121

W

We Two, Us 35
Winning Ticket 65
Wise Woman of the Rock, The 89

Y

Your Poem 49

www.ingramcontent.com/pod-product-compliance
Lightning Source LLC
Chambersburg PA
CBHW040016240426
43664CB00037B/39